MW01059925

the little book of
ZEN

Published by OH!
20 Mortimer Street
London W1T 3JW

Disclaimer:
This book and the information contained herein are for general educational and entertainment use only. The contents are not claimed to be exhaustive, and the book is sold on the understanding that neither the publishers nor the author are thereby engaged in rendering any kind of professional services. Users are encouraged to confirm the information contained herein with other sources and review the information carefully with their appropriate, qualified service providers. Neither the publishers nor the author shall have any responsibility to any person or entity regarding any loss or damage whatsoever, direct or indirect, consequential, special or exemplary, caused or alleged to be caused, by the use or misuse of information contained in this book.

ISBN 978-1-91161-092-2

Editorial consultant: Sasha Fenton
Editorial: Tina Chantrey, Victoria Godden
Project manager: Russell Porter
Design: Ben Ruocco
Production: Rachel Burgess

A CIP catalogue record for this book is available from the British Library

Printed in Dubai

10 9 8 7 6 5 4 3 2 1

Illustrations: Ditya Zemli/Shutterstock, piixypeach and Stockdevil/Freepik

the little book of
ZEN

tina chantrey

CONTENTS

Introduction   6

Chapter 1
What is zen?   8

Chapter 2
The benfits of zen   14

Chapter 3
What is meditation?   24

Chapter 4
Simple meditation
practices   44

Chapter 5
Zen-type quotations   90

Conclusion   190

INTRODUCTION

This book looks at the ancient practice known as Zen, and how it can be used today to improve every aspect of your life and wellbeing. It explains when and how the method first developed, and the principles on which it is based. The first part of the book covers meditation, while the second part supplies many well-known, and not so well-known, Zen-type affirmations and quotations for you to apply to everyday life. Zen quotes for living a full life will provide you with an endless resource for daily tasks and challenges. Whatever area of life you are having difficulties with, simply turn to the relevant chapter and you will find the inspiration and wisdom to sail through even the roughest of seas.

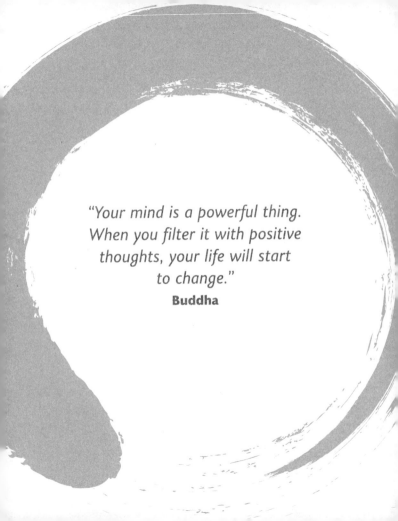

"Your mind is a powerful thing.
When you filter it with positive
thoughts, your life will start
to change."

Buddha

CHAPTER
1

WHAT
is ZEN?

In our ever-changing world, there is often only one thing that we can be assured of: that nothing ever stays the same. Finding a moment in your day to focus on the present, to ground yourself and to meditate can help you achieve a sense of peace. With our fast-paced lifestyles, many look to the ancient practice of Zen to find solace and understanding.

Zen is a type of Buddhist practice
that was first introduced into China
in the fifth century by the legendary
Bodhidharma. The beauty of Zen
Buddhism in our society is that it shows
that enlightenment can be reached
through meditation, self-contemplation
and intuition rather than through faith
or devotion.

Buddhism is widely practised in China, Japan, Korea and Vietnam, and we have all at some time read Zen quotes, whether in books, on fridge magnets or circulating on social media. They are everywhere we look, but now more than ever they can bring meaning to everyday life.

The word Zen is derived from the Japanese pronunciation (kana: ぜん) of the Chinese word 禅 (chán), which in turn comes from the words "meditative state". It evokes the most serene aspects of Japanese culture. It stands for rigorous self-restraint, meditation, and insight. It brings the personal expression of Zen insight into our daily life, and it encourages us to help others. It asks us to look to spiritual practice rather than religious doctrines.

CHAPTER

2

the
BENEFITS
of ZEN

By including a simple practice of daily Zen, you will experience a dramatically increased sense of calm. Zen helps reduce stress, anxiety and tension. Through this, your health and overall wellbeing will benefit. It can positively influence other everyday aspects of life too, from relationships to work and family issues. Learning how to remain in a calm and positive state while faced with adversity will help you find inner peace and happiness.

Zen helps you to acknowledge your thoughts as just that – the product of a mind that is endlessly creating new theories to keep itself busy. It enables you to let go of these thoughts and the judgements they create, and adopt a more explicit, more open and more understanding approach to life.

By being in a state of Zen, where you are focusing on correct breathing technique, you can release stress and anxiety. Many have found this can also help with dealing with physical pain.

Zen also allows you to gain a much deeper understanding of your own body and soul. By knowing yourself better, you achieve a state of calm, as well as gaining more insight into your capabilities. It's like turning off a noisy TV that has been buzzing away in the background, and suddenly feeling a wave of calm and quiet flowing into your mind.

Another benefit of regular Zen practice
is that it will increase your ability to
concentrate. Zen helps you clear your
mind so that you can focus on what is
essential in the present moment. It's at
these moments of clarity that creativity
can bubble up. It's like getting into the
"flow" or "zone" when you are taking
exercise because, at that moment, you
are no longer thinking of anything –
you're just allowing your body to move.

For instance, if you are running and you cross the finish line and have reached your personal best, you often don't know what you did differently; you just become aware that achieving this type of moving meditation can be extremely powerful. Usually, if you have a specific issue or problem to solve, by practising a state of Zen, you will find the solutions naturally come to you. Ignoring the distractions all around you, including technology, can lead to greater efficiency as well as allowing you to benefit from the peaceful state of achieving inner peace.

Many who adopt a Zen practice will also experience improved sleep. Achieving calm in your mind, body and spirit encourages more profound, more restful sleep. Many of us often get what feels like the perfect night's sleep after going to a yoga class in the evening, but with Zen meditation, you can achieve this every night!

Zen makes it easier to let go of worries and stresses that you realize aren't as significant as your mind wants you to believe they are. Getting into a deeper state of happiness also promotes better rest.

Self-doubt can lead you to underachieve. The Zen approach to life allows you to tackle your daily responsibilities from a more precise and more focused mind. It enables you to trust your ability to make decisions, as your mind becomes more accurate and attuned. And spending the time getting to know and trust yourself much more deeply can significantly boost your self-confidence.

CHAPTER
3

WHAT is MEDITATION?

Meditation covers a wide range of practices used in different traditions across cultures all over the world. As a term, it was introduced as a translation for Eastern spiritual practices, known as *dhyana* in Hinduism and Buddhism. This word has its roots in the Sanskrit word *dhyai*, meaning "to contemplate". There is no simple explanation of what it is, due to the different practices, but in general it means that a person uses a technique, such as mindfulness or focusing the mind, to achieve mental clarity and a calm state. Although used in antiquity, it was in the nineteenth century that Asian meditative techniques began to spread to other cultures.

Meditation may be used for many different reasons. Still, lots of practitioners turn to it to reduce stress and anxiety in their lives, as well as improve wellbeing. People also believe it has myriad health benefits.

Some meditation techniques suggest
a period of up to twenty minutes
of practice every day, while others
recommend much less, especially when
you are starting on your Zen journey.
The time of day you choose to meditate
can vary too, because some will prefer
to practice in the hours before dawn,
while others meditate at dusk. Often
people will fit in their time for meditation
much later in the day. especially if they
have family responsibilities.

There is no right or wrong way to meditate, and no right or wrong time or place for that matter – it simply must work for you. Many workplaces even offer mindfulness and meditation courses to reduce stress among employees, Google being a famous example.

Mindfulness in meditation aims to help you have a much healthier perspective; you're not trying to turn off thoughts and feelings, just learning to observe them without judgement.

Even though many of your thoughts and emotions can be upsetting and worrying, they come in waves and are fleeting. Meditation helps you to not react to your feelings. Trying to stop thoughts often makes them louder, while meditation enables you to quieten the chatter that goes on in your mind.

TIPS

Research shows that meditating for as little as ten minutes per day increases the brain's alpha waves, which are associated with relaxation, and helps combat anxiety and depression.

BREATHING

One way to practise Zen is by focusing
on your breathing and remaining in the
present moment. Create a relaxing place
to sit in an area free of distractions.
Some people like to light a candle,
while others sit in front of an altar using
objects that have meaning for them.
These can be flowers, stones, trinkets –
whatever makes the space restful.

TIPS

Whilst meditating, breathing deeply with slow and steady breaths will activate your parasympathetic nervous system to calm your body down. Long, deep breaths can also manage your stress responses.

While sitting on a small meditation cushion in the lotus position, try to regulate your mind by counting your breaths. Ensure you are comfortable, and your back is straight. Use pillows or cushions to prop up your back if you need to. More flexible people may find it comfortable to sit in the half-lotus position (hankafuza) or the full lotus position (kekkafuza).

To sit in the half-lotus position, place
your left foot onto your right thigh and
tuck your right leg under your left thigh.

For the full lotus, place each foot onto
the opposite thigh. Only try these
positions if you are pain-free.

Make sure there is no strain on your neck and that your head is in a natural position; imagine a straight line running up your spine and through the top of your head. Attach an imaginary helium balloon to the top of your head to continue the alignment of the spine and neck.

Relax all the tiny muscles in your neck, jaw and face. Allow your tongue to relax in your mouth and let go of any tension in the muscles of your forehead, around your eyes, your mouth and your jaw.

Breathe through your nose to create a
cooling and warming sensation as you
breathe in and out, and to help you
create a gentle rhythm. Place all your
focus on your breath and concentrate
on every inhalation and exhalation.
Feel the air travelling in through your
nose and into your lungs before it leaves
your body again. Focus on the sound of
your breathing. Strive to put your full
awareness onto your breath as you begin
to meditate.

You are also aiming to silence the mind. So, every time a thought pops into your mind, imagine letting it float away like a cloud on a breeze. Put your focus back on your breath. If another thought bubbles up, repeat this practice of imagining the idea drifting away and return your focus to your breath.

It sounds simple, but it can take a lot of practice to quieten your mind. If you struggle to focus on your breath, don't be disillusioned, because meditation, like all things, takes practice. Start with a two-minute exercise, and as you find it easier to center on your breath and calm your mind, you can try to meditate for longer.

Try to shut your eyes, or if you prefer them to be open, focus on one spot in your room. If your eyes start to wander, close them and refocus on your breath. Every time your mind begins to wander, redirect it to focusing on your breathing.

Imagine your lungs as a radio that you are trying to tune and keep focusing on the in and out of your breath. It may help to count your breaths.

Start gradually, with just a few minutes of meditation, and then slowly increase the time as you get better at focusing on your breath and quietening your mind. You are not trying to achieve perfection, so it doesn't matter how long you meditate when you start, since it will eventually become more natural.

Once you have set up a Zen meditation routine, you can turn to this book at the end of your meditation. Either let the book open before you and read the quote on that page, or find a section to which you feel drawn, and learn from that.

Whenever you feel lethargic, disillusioned, stressed or angry, you have fallen out of alignment with your true inner self. Turn to these Zen sayings to help you achieve inner peace and calm along with all the other health and wellness benefits this can lead to in our ever-changing world.

CHAPTER

4

SIMPLE
MEDITATION
PRACTICES

A meditative practice allows an individual to focus the mind. It may involve concentrating on one subject intensely for a prolonged time, often the breath. When we achieve a deep state of calm, by focusing on the breath, this may also allow you to reach a high level of spiritual awareness.

Creating time in each day for meditation will bring bliss into your life. Remember, meditation requires nothing except present-moment awareness. There is no right or wrong way to meditate; anything and everything you do will be beneficial. What follows are some simple meditation methods to try for yourself.

simple daily
MEDITATION
practice for
BEGINNERS

Find a quiet space where you have the least chance of being disturbed.

Make yourself comfortable by either sitting on a cushion or lying down on the floor on your back, with your feet on the floor and your knees bent.

Aim for just two minutes and slowly work up to ten minutes. Remember, don't force yourself to meditate for longer than feels comfortable; it's not a race, rather a gradual progression.

Put your left hand in the middle of your chest and your right hand on your solar plexus area, on your belly under your ribcage. Relax your elbows next to your body. Start by focusing on your breath and listening to the in-and-out flow as you breathe. Don't try to control your breathing, just observe the air going in and out of your body.

As you feel yourself relax, begin to take deeper in-breaths – slow down your breathing and sense your right hand rise as you take each breath deep into your lungs. As you exhale, slow down the out-breath as you feel the air leave your body.

You can bring in some visualization, if you like. So while you breathe in for a count of four, imagine the air coming into your lungs bringing in warm energy. Feel this warm, energized air travelling through your body right to the tips of your fingers and toes. As you exhale, imagine relaxing all the muscles in your body, from your feet to your scalp, and letting go of any tension you may be holding in them.

With every inhale and exhale, listen to the sound of your breath and feel your hands rise and fall. Imagine the warm, energizing air travelling through your body, relaxing all your muscles on its journey.

If you lose your concentration and your mind starts to wander, acknowledge this without judgement and bring your attention back to your breath as it rises and falls.

You may want to chant a mantra in your head to help your mind settle. Think of a positive emotion, a feeling or state you would like to focus on, such as being healthy, strong, calm or joyous. Then, repeat your mantra over and over, inserting the word you have chosen, after the words "I am". For example "I am healthy."

It may be a good idea to set a timer for two minutes to start with. Then, when the time has elapsed, you can take your time to allow your attention to come back to the present before gently getting up and going about your daily life. Each time you meditate from then on, try to add another minute to your session.

a simple
MEDITATION
for busy
PARENTS

With a full and challenging day,
it may be easier for parents
to fit in a meditation practice
earlier in the day.

Getting up earlier may offer busy mums and dads the best opportunity to meditate, before wakeful energy infuses the household and time for themselves gets lost in the countless jobs that need their attention.

This doesn't mean you have to get up when it's still dark, just aim for twenty minutes before your children wake up. The great advantage of early-morning meditation is that it gives you a precious moment in your day when you can tune into your thoughts before the daily chaos begins.

Find yourself a comfortable and peaceful space. This could be your bed, though it may be an idea to get up and change position to ensure your body and mind don't drift back to sleep. If you choose to sit on a meditation cushion next to your bed, ensure you are sitting upright. Now imagine you have a helium balloon on a piece of string coming out of the top of your head.

Place your focus on your breath and feel
the inward and outward flow of air from
your body. Begin a body scan, starting
with your feet. How are they feeling?
Slowly move your awareness up your
body to check how each part is feeling.
Place your awareness in your mind. How
does it feel? Are you anxious or worried
about something that is coming in your
day? Is your mind feeling relaxed, or tired?

Don't examine these feelings; just acknowledge they are there. Focus again on your breathing and, without forcing it, try to slow it down. Breathe deeply into the bottom of your lungs, and before you breathe out, feel the space between the in-and-out breath. When you breathe out, ensure you empty the whole of your lungs.

If your mind begins to wander, that's
all right. Don't criticize yourself when
thoughts start to pop into your mind.
Instead simply acknowledge their
presence, let them go and try to refocus
on your breath. Remember, there's
no right or wrong way to meditate.
Even a few minutes of practice every
day will help you stay more focused
in the present moment and feel less
susceptible to worries about the future
or feelings from the past.

Another perfect time to meditate is when you are going to bed, as it can allow you to "download" the day and let go of any worries or anxieties that may have bubbled up. One issue with this is that, as tired parents, you may find that your meditation sends you straight to sleep!

Remember, when your day is hectic, being flexible about when and how to meditate is vital. Grounding yourself and connecting to your core each day can help alleviate stress. Even if you find it challenging to make time for yourself, you can work on your breathing anytime, anywhere.

Deep yogic breaths, where your chest and then stomach expand as you breathe deeply into your lungs, can significantly revitalize you. On the exhale, release your breath slowly from your throat area, then your chest, and finally your stomach. Just ten repetitions can create a feeling of calm and deep relaxation, helping you release tension and return to a sense of peacefulness. Why not get your children to do this with you during the day? That way they can share your practice and benefit too.

a simple

MEDITATION

practice for

WORKERS

However busy you are at work, taking just five minutes out of your schedule can create an instant state of calm and allow you to be more productive.

Whatever pressures you may be under, taking a short time just to focus on your breath, conducting a simple body scan and letting go of thoughts as though they were in a balloon drifting up into the sky, will bring calmness, clarity and, hopefully, happiness.

Make sure you are somewhere quiet. The workplace can often be stressful, so even if you only have a few minutes, ensure you are somewhere with the best chance of not being disturbed. Turn off your phone. Try to choose the same time to meditate every day, so that it becomes a habit.

It may be easier to do a walking
meditation during your working day,
where you spend ten to fifteen minutes
out of the office. If you can't manage
this, start by spending a few minutes
focusing on your breath. Sitting
comfortably, close your eyes and take
long, deep, even breaths, in through
your nose and out through your mouth.
Be aware of the space around you.
As you breathe in, feel the fresh air
entering your body through your nose.

Every time you breathe out, let go of any stress in the body and mind. Allow your thoughts to come and go. Feel your muscles soften every time you breathe out, and sense how your feet connect to the ground. Be aware of how your body feels, starting at your feet and working your way up to your head.

If you come across any tension or stress, let go of it as you exhale. Then spend a few moments noticing how your mind feels. Are you stressed or anxious, for example or calm and collected? As you breathe out, let go of any negative feelings.

Spend a few minutes focusing on the
rise and fall of your breath. If your mind
wanders, that's fine. Gently bring your
attention back to the breath, and then
your body. Become aware of how your
body is feeling now you have let go of
your stress and tension. Then, when
you're ready, gently open your eyes and
slowly stand up.

Meditation will help you to discipline yourself at work, which will permeate into your daily routine. It will help you focus on your work and feel more productive, as well as reducing frustration. It may also help you feel more compassionate towards your colleagues, making working as a team easier and boosting your overall sense of job satisfaction.

simple

MEDITATION

for

STRESS

Find a quiet space where
you can step away from
your busy day.

Make yourself comfortable. Either sit down on a meditation cushion or lie down on the floor on your back, with your knees bent and your feet on the floor.

Close your eyes and take a few moments to tune into your breath. Then take a few moments to tune into your body. Notice any tension or stress you may be holding in your muscles – where is it? Or are you feeling anxious in your mind? Don't judge yourself for these feelings or try to solve them; just acknowledge they are there.

Focus on your breath and allow your mind to settle slowly. As thoughts pop into your mind, acknowledge them and then let them go like a cloud drifting away in the sky. Breathe in for a count of four and out for a count of six, taking the in-breath deep into the bottom of your lungs, and letting the out-breath completely empty your lungs.

As you breathe in, invite in the thought "breathing in calm". As you exhale, invite the idea: "letting go" or: "letting go of stress" or "letting go of the day". Begin with just a few minutes, and then try to add one minute every time you meditate. When you have finished, take your time as you stand up.

simple

MEDITATION

for

CHILDREN

A simple, short daily
meditation practice can boost
your child's immune system.

There are several methods you can teach your child that will help them slow down their minds and improve their health.

A simple body and mind check-in will take just a few moments, but can be hugely beneficial. Encourage them to ask themselves what feelings they are experiencing. Ask them to consider what their emotions feel like in their body.

For example, if they are nervous, ask
them how that feels in their body. What
about when they are excited? Or sad?
Ask them how it feels in their body.
This helps children to reach a deeper
understanding of their thoughts and
feelings, and the way that these can
affect their bodies. It also helps them to
understand that emotions can come in
waves and that they can leave as quickly
as they arrive.

The practice of mindfulness is another fun way for children to stay in the present, and to be aware of their thoughts, feelings and physical sensations. This can take any form. For example, when your child next has a bath or shower, encourage them to have a "mindful" bath or shower.

Ask them to listen to the water, to notice how it feels on their skin all over their body, to watch the water draining down their legs, over the feet and away. Mindfulness is a complex concept for young children, but asking them to listen, see and feel their surroundings is easy and can even be fun.

Practising relaxation at bedtime can help children settle after a busy day. At the end of their bedtime routine of, say, bath, pyjamas and a story, introduce a body scan while focusing on deep breathing – you can help them slip into a calmer state, ready for sleep.

When they are lying down, ask them to focus on their toes and feet and to relax all the muscles in this area. Slowly work your way up their body, helping them to focus on that limb or muscle group while they take slower, deeper breaths, and to let each area relax. Finish with their neck and shoulders, and then their face. Don't forget to ask them to rest their forehead, the tiny muscles around their eyes, their cheeks, their jaw and their tongue.

Finish the body scan and take a few deep breaths to finish the relaxation. Both parent and child will then be in a much calmer place.

simple

MEDITATION

practice for

ACTIVE PEOPLE

If you've tried meditation at home and have struggled to sit still or quieten the voices in your head, you may benefit more from movement meditation.

Your body doesn't have to be physically still for you to receive help from meditation. Movement meditation also helps you appreciate the beauty of the natural world, while slow, repetitive movements can help calm your mind.

This form of meditation may include walking through a park, fields or forest, or by the sea, or it can consist of gardening or even running. It is a more active form of meditation where movement helps you quieten your mind and focus on the present moment, as well as helping to release physical tension.

When you do movement meditation,
you feel the sensations in your body.
These can begin with noticing the
sensation of your breath. Then feel
your feet against the earth, noticing
how the shoes you are wearing feel
while you listen to the sounds they
make as you move.

If you are walking, place your focus on
your arm movements. Notice how your
hands, elbows and shoulders feel as
your arms move, and how the air may
be brushing against them. You may find
you coordinate your arm movement
with your breath.

This is an opportunity to focus your attention on parts of the body you generally ignore. How do your feet feel as they hit the ground? Are your toes scrunched up or relaxed and splayed apart? Perform a complete body scan to enable you to tune into every part of your body rather than those you usually notice, such as your hands. Feel the glutes in your bottom working, feel your belly moving, so that you get a sense of your physical whole.

Make sure you focus on the movement, rather than where you may be going. If you are jogging, listen to the rhythm of your footfalls and allow your breath to coordinate with them if it wishes to. See your environment, be aware of the taste of the air as it enters your mouth, feel your arms rubbing against your body.

WHEN you SHOULDN'T MEDITATE

Meditation isn't for everyone; those who are suffering from severe depression or other mental health problems can find that meditation releases difficult emotions and feelings.

Some may have an extreme reaction. Although this may be rare, if you are suffering from severe anxiety or depression, you should discuss your suitability for this practice with your doctor first.

By becoming more in touch with your feelings, suppressed or hidden emotions may lead to feelings of anger, sadness or fear. It's essential if you experience these feelings that you are compassionate towards yourself.

If you are feeling a sense of imbalance or loss of identity, step away from meditation until you feel healthy, and seek medical help. As with all complementary therapies, even though many people around the world find meditation helpful, there can be downsides.

CHAPTER
5

ZEN-TYPE QUOTATIONS

This part of the book is filled with Zen-type quotations that will help you cope with many of life's difficulties. They are arranged by topic, so just choose the one that seems to fit your circumstances and absorb the Zen wisdom that is here for you.

"When the student is ready, the teacher will appear."
Zen Proverb

"Only when you can be extremely pliable and soft can you be tough and strong."
Zen Proverb

INSPIRATION
and
MOTIVATION

"The most important thing in life is to stop saying 'I wish' and start saying 'I will'. Consider nothing impossible, and then treat possibilities as probabilities."

Charles Dickens

"When it is obvious that the goals cannot be reached, don't adjust the goals, adjust the action steps."

Confucius

"Dare to live the life you have dreamed for yourself. Go forward and make your dreams come true."

Ralph Waldo Emerson

"Life is not always a matter of holding good cards, but sometimes, playing a poor hand well."

Jack London

"Travel brings power and love back into your life."

Rumi

"Failure is only the opportunity to begin again, this time more intelligently."
Henry Ford

"Have a mind that is open to everything and attached to nothing."
Tilopa

"The future belongs to those who believe in the beauty of their dreams."
Eleanor Roosevelt

"Yesterday I was clever, so I wanted to change the world. Today I am wise, so I am changing myself."
Rumi

"It is the power of the mind to be unconquerable."
Seneca

"It is not the strongest of the species that survive, or the most intelligent, but the one most responsive to change."
Charles Darwin

"Begin doing what you want to do now. We are not living in eternity. We have only this moment, sparkling like a star in our hand and melting like a snowflake."

Francis Bacon, Sr.

"If you want happiness for a year, inherit a fortune. If you want happiness for a lifetime, help someone else."

Confucius

"Without ambition, one starts nothing. Without work, one finishes nothing. The prize will not be sent to you. You have to win it."

Ralph Waldo Emerson

"It is never too late to be what you might have been."
George Eliot

"Defeat is not the worst of failures. Not to have tried is the true failure."
George Edward Woodberry

"You are not meant for crawling, so don't. You have wings. Learn to use them and fly."
Rumi

"You must be the change you wish
to see in the world."
Mahatma Gandhi

"Make the best use of what's
in your power and take the rest
as it happens."
Epictetus

"He who has a why to live can bear
almost any how."
Friedrich Nietzsche

HEALTH

"To keep the body in good health is a duty, for otherwise we shall not be able to trim the lamp of wisdom, and keep our mind strong and clear."

Buddha

"Health is the greatest gift, contentment the greatest wealth, faithfulness the best relationship."

Buddha

"Health is the greatest possession. Contentment is the greatest treasure. Confidence is the greatest friend. Non-being is the greatest joy."

Lao Tzu

"He who has health has hope; and he who has hope has everything."

Arabian Proverb

*"The best cure for the body is
a quiet mind."*
Napoleon Bonaparte

*"It is health that is real wealth and
not pieces of gold and silver."*
Mahatma Gandhi

WISDOM

"You are exactly where you
need to be."
Anonymous

"Life is a balance of holding
on and letting go."
Rumi

"The quieter you become, the more you can hear."
Lao Tzu

"Knowing others is intelligence; knowing yourself is true wisdom. Mastering others is strength; mastering yourself is true power."
Lao Tzu

"The worst of all deceptions
is self-deception."
Plato

"Reflect upon your present blessings –
of which every man has many –
not on your past misfortunes,
of which all men have some."
Charles Dickens

"Knowledge is learning something every day. Wisdom is letting go of something every day."

Anonymous

"As a bee gathering nectar does not harm or disturb the colour and fragrance of the flower; so, do the wise move through the world."

Buddha

"As soon as you trust yourself, you will know how to live."

Johann Wolfgang von Goethe

"The gem cannot be polished without friction, nor man perfected without trials."
Chinese Proverb

"No bird soars too high, if he soars with his own wings."
William Blake

"Taking a new step, uttering a new word, are what people fear most."
Fyodor Dostoevsky

"Choose a job you love, and you will never have to work a day in your life."
Confucius

"If you are filled with pride, then you will have no room for wisdom."
African Proverb

"Those who are free of resentful thoughts surely find peace."
Buddha

"If you cry because the sun has gone out of your life, your tears will prevent you from seeing the stars."
Rabindranath Tagore

"If you want to travel the Way of Buddhas and Zen masters, then expect nothing, seek nothing, and grasp nothing."
Dōgen Zenji

"Simplicity is the ultimate sophistication."
Leonardo da Vinci

"When one door closes, another opens; but we often look so long and so regretfully upon the closed door that we do not see the one that has opened for us."
Alexander Graham Bell

"The wise man looks back into the past, and does not grieve over what is far off, nor rejoice over what is near; for he knows that time is without end."

Lao Tzu

"No man ever steps in the same river twice, for it's not the same river and he's not the same man."

Heraclitus

overflowing
CUP OF TEA

*"Out beyond ideas of wrongdoing
and right doing, there is a field. I'll
meet you there. When the soul lies
down in that grass, the world is too
full to talk about."*

Rumi

*"The Zen Master poured his visitor's teacup
full, and then kept pouring. The visitor
watched until he could no longer restrain
himself. "It is overfull. No more will go
in!" "Like this cup," the Zen Master said,
"you are full of your own opinions and
assumptions. How can you learn the truth
until you first empty your cup?"*

Traditional Zen Koan

LIFE
and
HAPPINESS

"Why do you so earnestly seek the truth in distant places? Look for delusion and truth in the bottom of your own heart."

Ryōkan

"Change is never painful, only the resistance to change is painful."

Buddha

"The glory of friendship is not the outstretched hand, not the kindly smile, nor the joy of companionship; it is the spiritual inspiration that comes to one when you discover that someone else believes in you and is willing to trust you with a friendship."

Ralph Waldo Emerson

"In one's family, respect and listening are the sources of harmony."

Buddha

"There is no duty more obligatory than the repayment of kindness."

Cicero

"Do not say, 'It is morning,' and dismiss it with a name of yesterday. See it for the first time as a newborn child that has no name."

Rabindranath Tagore

"The greatest effort is not concerned with results."

Atisa

"Live as if you were to die tomorrow. Learn as if you were to live forever."

Mahatma Gandhi

*"The greater the difficulty,
the more glory in surmounting it.
Skilful pilots gain their reputation
from storms and tempests."*

Epictetus

*"Walk away from anything or anyone
who takes away from your joy. Life is
too short to put up with fools."*

Anonymous

*"To live is the rarest thing in the
world. Most people exist, that is all."*

Oscar Wilde

"Happiness is a gift and the trick is
not to expect it, but to delight in it
when it comes."
Charles Dickens

"When walking, walk.
When eating, eat."
Zen proverb

"The two most important days in your
life are the day you are born, and the
day you find out why."
Mark Twain

"The way to happiness is: keep your heart free from hate, your mind from worry. Live simply, give much. Fill your life with love. Do as you would be done by."

Buddha

"Do not look for a sanctuary in anyone except yourself."

Buddha

"There is no duty we so much underrate as the duty of being happy. By being happy, we sow anonymous benefits upon the world."

Robert Louis Stevenson

"Laugh as much as you breathe. Love as long as you live."

Rumi

"Do not go where the path may lead, go instead where there is no path and leave a trail."

Ralph Waldo Emerson

"When the spirits are low, when the day appears dark, when work becomes monotonous, when hope hardly seems worth having, just mount a bicycle and go out for a spin down the road, without thought on anything but the ride you are taking."

Arthur Conan Doyle

"In business, reinvest a portion of all you make, keep a portion for your use, save a portion for those in need."
Buddha

"You must live in the present, launch yourself on every wave, find your eternity in each moment. Fools stand on their island of opportunities and look toward another land. There is no other land; there is no other life but this."
Henry David Thoreau

"Chance is always powerful. Let your hook be always cast; in the pool where you least expect it, there will be a fish."

Ovid

"How much better is silence; the coffee cup, the table. How much better to sit by myself like the solitary sea-bird that opens its wings on the stake."

Virginia Woolf

"Thousands of candles can be lighted from a single candle, and the life of the candle will not be shortened. Happiness never decreases by being shared."

Buddha

"The way out is through the door. Why is it that no one will use this method?"

Confucius

"Maybe you are searching among the branches for what only appears in the roots."

Rumi

"In the end, it's not the years in your life that count. It's the life in your years."

Abraham Lincoln

"*Be content with what you have; rejoice in the way things are. When you realize nothing is lacking, the whole world belongs to you.*"

Lao Tzu

"*Man is fond of counting his troubles, but he does not count his joys. If he counted them up, as he ought to, he would see that every lot has enough happiness provided for it.*"

Fyodor Dostoevsky

"*You are today where your thoughts have brought you; you will be tomorrow where your thoughts take you.*"

James Allen

SELF-BELIEF
and
SELF-LOVE

"Balance is the perfect state of still water. Let that be our model. It remains quiet within and is not disturbed on the surface."
Confucius

"Magic is believing in yourself; if you can do that, you can make anything happen."
Johann Wolfgang von Goethe

"Conventional opinion is the ruin of our souls."
Rumi

"Work out your own salvation. Do not depend on others."
Buddha

"Do not judge yourself harshly. Without mercy for ourselves, we cannot love the world."
Buddha

132

"Out of your vulnerabilities will come your strength."
Sigmund Freud

"If you cannot find a good companion to walk with, walk alone, like an elephant roaming the jungle. It is better to be alone than to be with those who will hinder your progress."
Buddha

"Your treasure house is in yourself; it contains all you need."
Hui Hai

"To thine own self be true."
William Shakespeare

*"Flow with whatever may happen,
and let your mind be free: Stay
centred by accepting whatever you
are doing. This is the ultimate."*
Chuang-Tzu

*"Don't judge each day by the harvest
you reap but by the seeds that you
plant. To be what we are, and to
become what we are capable of
becoming, is the only end of life."*
Robert Stevenson

"One ought, every day at least, to hear a little song, read a good poem, see a fine picture, and, if it were possible, to speak a few reasonable words."

Johann Wolfgang von Goethe

"When you are content to simply be yourself and don't compare or compete, everybody will respect you."

Lao Tzu

"To be yourself in a world that is constantly trying to make you something else is the greatest accomplishment."

Ralph Waldo Emerson

"*To love oneself is the beginning of a lifelong romance.*"

Oscar Wilde

"*I want to sing like the birds sing, not worrying about who hears or what they think.*"

Rumi

"*Be ye lamps unto yourselves. Be your own reliance. Hold to the truth within yourselves as to the only lamp.*"

Buddha

"You can search throughout the entire
universe for someone more deserving
of your love and affection than you
are yourself, and that person is not to
be found anywhere. You, yourself, as
much as anybody in the entire universe,
deserve your love and affection."
Buddha

"To know what you prefer instead of
humbly saying Amen to what the world
says you ought to prefer, is to have
kept your soul alive."
Robert Stevenson

"What lies behind us and what lies before us are tiny matters, compared to what lies within us."

Ralph Waldo Emerson

"First they ignore you, then they laugh at you, then they fight you, then you win."

Mahatma Gandhi

"No need to hurry. No need to sparkle. No need to be anybody but oneself."

Virginia Woolf

"Do not follow the idea of others,
but learn to listen to the voice
within yourself."
Dōgen Zenji

"Work out your own salvation.
Do not depend on others."
Confucius

"When I let go of what I am,
I become what I might be."
Lao Tzu

LEARNING

*"Education breeds confidence.
Confidence breeds hope. Hope
breeds peace."*
Confucius

*"One day, in retrospect,
the years of struggle will strike
you as the most beautiful."*
Sigmund Freud

"Have the fearless attitude of a hero and the loving heart of a child."
Soyen Shaku

"A book is like a garden, carried in the pocket."
Chinese Proverb

"To the mind that is still, the whole universe surrenders."
Lao Tzu

"*Do not learn how to react. Learn how to respond.*"

Buddha

"*A child who reads will be an adult who thinks.*"

Anonymous

"*Every experience, no matter how bad it seems, holds within a blessing of some kind. The goal is to find it.*"

Buddha

"Books are the bees which carry the quickening pollen from one to another mind."
James Russell Lowell

"No matter how busy you may think you are, you must find time for reading, or surrender yourself to self-chosen ignorance."
Confucius

"Once you learn to read, you will forever be free."
Frederick Douglass

"To read a book for the first time is to make an acquaintance with a new friend; to read it for a second time is to meet an old one."
Chinese Saying

"To think is easy. To act is hard. But the hardest thing in the world is to act by following your thinking."
Johann Wolfgang von Goethe

"The journey of a thousand miles begins with one step."
Lao Tzu

LOVE
and
COMPASSION

"Love is not love which alters when it alteration finds... it is an ever-fixed mark."
William Shakespeare

"A man sees in the world what he carries in his heart."
Johann Wolfgang von Goethe

"It is only with the heart that one can see rightly; what is essential is invisible to the eye."
Antoine de Saint-Exupéry

"Only from the heart can you touch the sky."

Rumi

"Our sorrows and wounds are only healed when we touch them with compassion."

Buddha

"If you look into your own heart, and you find nothing wrong there, what is there to worry about? What is there to fear?"

Confucius

"My dear heart, never think you are better than others. Listen to their sorrows with compassion. If you want peace, don't harbour bad thoughts, do not gossip and don't teach what you do not know."

Rumi

"He who loves with purity considers not the gift of the lover, but the love of the giver."

Thomas Kempis

ANXIETY
and
DEPRESSION

"If you are depressed, you are
living in the past. If you are anxious,
you are living in the future. If you are
at peace, you are living
in the present."
Lao Tzu

"The biggest obstacle
you'll ever have to overcome is your
mind. If you can overcome that, you
can overcome anything."
Anonymous

"In the midst of chaos, there is also opportunity."
Sun Tzu

"Once you stop clinging and let things be, you'll be free, even of birth and death. You'll transform everything."
Bodhidharma

"People become attached to their burdens sometimes more than the burdens are attached to them."
George Bernard Shaw

"You wouldn't worry so much about what others think of you if you realized how seldom they do."
Eleanor Roosevelt

"Worrying doesn't take away tomorrow's troubles; it takes away today's peace."
Anonymous

"Be content with what you have; rejoice in the way things are. When you realize there is nothing lacking, the whole world belongs to you."
Lao Tzu

"Trouble is a tunnel through which we pass and not a brick wall against which we must break through."
Chinese Proverb

"Worry often gives a small thing a big shadow."
Swedish Proverb

Anger, Ignorance and Injustice
"To be wronged is nothing unless you continue to remember it."
Confucius

"Anger is like a thorn in the heart."
Yiddish Proverb

"Once you know the nature of anger and joy is empty and you let them go, you free yourself from karma."
Buddha

"Life is too short to argue and fight with the past. Count your blessings, value your loved ones, and move on with your head held high."
Anonymous

"We are not disturbed by what happens to us, but by our thoughts about what happens to us."
Epictetus

"There is nothing more frightful than ignorance in action."
Johann Wolfgang von Goethe

"Keep your fears to yourself, but share your courage with others."
Robert Louis Stevenson

"If you let cloudy water settle, it will become clear. If you let your upset mind settle, your course will also become clear."

Buddha

"It is useless to meet revenge with revenge; it will heal nothing."

J. R. R. Tolkien

"None are more hopelessly enslaved than those who falsely believe they are free."

Johann Wolfgang von Goethe

"Inner peace begins the moment you choose not to allow another person or event to control your emotions."

Anonymous

"Those who are free of resentful thoughts surely find peace."

Buddha

"No act of kindness, however small, is ever wasted."

Aesop

"If you know something hurtful and not true, don't say it. If you know something hurtful and true, don't say it. If you know something helpful but not true, don't say it. If you know something helpful and true, find the right time to say it."

Buddha

"In taking revenge, a man is but even with his enemy; but in passing it over, he is superior."

Francis Bacon, Sr

"Arrogance means that one knows how to press forward but not how to draw back, that one knows existence but not annihilation, knows something about winning but nothing about losing."

I Ching

"We can easily forgive a child who is afraid of the dark; the real tragedy of life is when men are afraid of the light."

Plato

"As rain falls equally on the just and the unjust, do not burden your heart with judgments but rain your kindness equally on all."

Buddha

"In this world, hate never yet dispelled hate. Only love dispels hate. This is the law, ancient and inexhaustible."

Buddha

"Justice means minding one's own business and not meddling with other men's concerns."

Plato

FORGIVENESS

"It is better to conquer yourself than to win a thousand battles. Then the victory is yours. It cannot be taken from you, not by angels or by demons, heaven or hell."

Buddha

"Forgive and be free. Forget that you have forgiven and be freer."

Buddha

"Sometimes it's better to be kind than to be right. We do not need an intelligent mind that speaks, but a patient heart that listens. You will not be punished for your anger; you will be punished by your anger."
Buddha

"Nothing is so praiseworthy, nothing so clearly shows a great and noble soul, as clemency and readiness to forgive."
Marcus Cicero

*"Peace comes from within.
Do not seek it without."*
Buddha

*"Forgiveness is the fragrance
that the violet sheds on the heel
that has crushed it."*
Mark Twain

"Healing is a matter of time,
but it is sometimes also a matter
of opportunity."
Hippocrates

"He who cannot forgive breaks
the bridge over which he himself
must pass."
George Herbert

"I have always found that mercy bears richer fruits than strict justice."
Abraham Lincoln

"There is nothing more dreadful than the habit of doubt. Doubt separates people. It is a poison that disintegrates friendships and breaks up pleasant relations; it is a thorn that irritates and hurts; it is a sword that kills."
Buddha

"Sometimes, when things are falling apart, they may actually be falling into place."
Anonymous

"Everything we hear is an opinion, not a fact. Everything we see is a perspective, not the truth."
Marcus Aurelius

"Holding on to anger is like grasping a hot coal with the intent of throwing it at someone else; you are the one who gets burned."
Buddha

"Hating someone makes them important. Forgiving them makes them obsolete."

Anonymous

"To understand everything is to forgive everything."

Buddha

NATURE

"Nature does not hurry, yet everything is accomplished."
Lao Tzu

"Things derive their being and nature by mutual dependence and are nothing in themselves."
Nagarjuna

"Just living is not enough... one must have sunshine, freedom, and a little flower."
Hans Christian Andersen

"The earth laughs in flowers."
Ralph Waldo Emerson

"It is not so much for its beauty that the forest makes a claim upon men's hearts, as for that subtle something, that quality of air that emanation from old trees, that so wonderfully changes and renews a weary spirit."
Robert Louis Stevenson

"Adopt the pace of nature: her secret is patience."
Ralph Waldo Emerson

"The least movement is of importance to all nature. The entire ocean is affected by a pebble."
Blaise Pascal

"The poetry of the earth is never dead."
John Keats

"I go to nature to be soothed and healed, and to have my senses put in order."
John Burroughs

"Nature never did betray the heart that loved her."
William Wordsworth

"Water, everywhere over the earth, flows to join together. A single natural law controls it. Each human is a member of a community and should work within it."
I Ching

"In every walk with nature, one receives far more than he seeks."
John Muir

"The sun does not shine for a few trees and flowers, but for the wide world's joy."

Henry Ward Beecher

"The sun himself is weak when he first rises, and gathers strength and courage as the day gets on."

Charles Dickens

"Nothing ever exists entirely alone. Everything is in relation to everything else."

Buddha

SPIRITUALITY

"I have been a seeker, and I still am,
but I stopped asking the books and
the stars. I started listening to the
teaching of my soul."

Rumi

"Allow yourself to rest. Your soul
speaks to you in the quiet moments in
between your thoughts."

Anonymous

"To the mind that is still, the whole universe surrenders."

Lao Tzu

"You should sit in meditation for twenty minutes every day. Unless you are too busy – then you should sit for an hour."

Old Zen Adage

"Serenity comes when you trade expectations for acceptance."

Buddha

"Let go of your mind and then be mindful. Close your ears and listen!"
Rumi

"See and realize that this world is not permanent. Neither late nor early flowers will remain."
Ryōkan

"When you do things from your soul, you feel a river moving in you, a joy."
Rumi

"Time's the king of men; he's both their parent, and he is their grave, and gives them what he will, not what they crave."
William Shakespeare

"We carry inside us the wonders we seek outside us."
Rumi

"The whole moon and the entire sky are reflected in one dewdrop on the grass."
Dōgen Zenji

"When I am silent, I fall into the place where everything is music."
Rumi

"Let your mind wander in the pure and simple. Be one with the infinite. Let all things take their course."
Chuang Tzu

LOSS,
GRIEF
and
DEATH

"Whenever sorrow comes, be kind to it. For God has placed a pearl in sorrow's hand."

Rumi

"Friends show their love in times of trouble, not in happiness."

Euripides

"*Even death is not to be feared by one who has lived wisely.*"
Buddha

"*Grief is the agony of an instant; the indulgence of grief the blunder of a life.*"
Benjamin Disraeli

"*Pain is certain: suffering is optional.*"
Buddha

"Like a bird singing in the rain, let grateful memories survive in time of sorrow."
Robert Louis Stevenson

"I learned that every mortal will taste death. But only some will taste life."
Rumi

"Death must be so beautiful. To lie in the soft brown earth, with the grasses waving above one's head, and listen to silence. To have no yesterday, and no tomorrow. To forget time, to forgive life, to be at peace."
Oscar Wilde

"Grief never mended no broken bones."

Charles Dickens

"Let go over a cliff, die completely, and then come back to life — after that, you cannot be deceived."

Zen Proverb

"Death has nothing to do with going away. The sun sets. The moon sets. But they are not gone."

Rumi

"How do you move on? You move on
when your heart finally understands
that there is no turning back."
J. R. R. Tolkien

"Sorrow... It pulls up the rotten roots
so that new roots hidden beneath
have room to grow. Whatever sorrow
shakes from your heart, far better
things will take their place."
Rumi

"If you realize that all things change, there is nothing you will try to hold on to. If you are not afraid of dying, there is nothing you cannot achieve."
Lao Tzu

"Into each life some rain must fall."
Henry Wadsworth Longfellow

*"Don't curse the darkness,
light a candle."*
Confucius

*"We never understand how little we
need in this world until we know
the loss of it."*
Sir James Matthew Barrie

CONCLUSION

These Zen sayings, as well as introducing a simple Zen practice into your everyday life, can significantly improve your health and wellbeing. Dip into this book daily, either by picking a random page or looking up a subject close to your heart. The benefits of following the wisdom of Zen, in healing mind, body and spirit, will help you achieve a new level of inner peace and calm and a new-found way to live a more centred life.

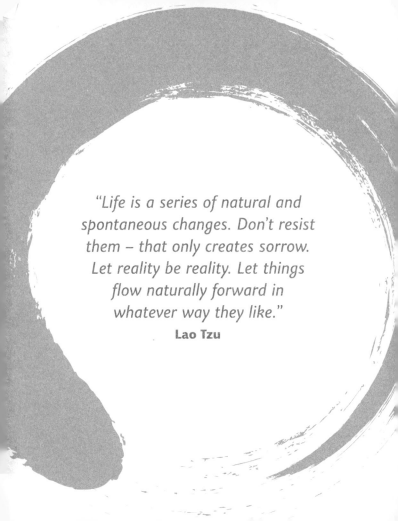

"*Life is a series of natural and spontaneous changes. Don't resist them – that only creates sorrow. Let reality be reality. Let things flow naturally forward in whatever way they like.*"

Lao Tzu

"*Each morning
we are born again.
What we do today
is what matters most.*"

Buddha